CENTRAL DIVISION

CHICAGO BLACKHAWKS
nickname: Hawks
team colors: red, black and white
home arena: United Center
mascot: Tommy Hawk
Stanley Cups won: 4

COLUMBUS BLUE JACKETS
nickname: Jackets
team colors: blue, red and green
home arena: Nationwide Arena
mascot: Stinger

DETROIT RED WINGS
nickname: Wings
team colors: red and white
home arena: Joe Louis Arena
mascot (unofficial): Al the octopus
Stanley Cups won: 11

NASHVILLE PREDATORS
nickname: Preds
team colors: navy blue, silver, white and gold
home arena: Sommet Center
mascot: Gnash

ST. LOUIS BLUES
team colors: white, navy blue and gold
home arena: Scottrade Center

NORTHWEST DIVISION

CALGARY FLAMES
team colors: red, gold, black and white
home arena: Pengrowth Saddledome
mascot: Harvey the Hound
Stanley Cups won: 1

COLORADO AVALANCHE
nickname: Avs
team colors: burgundy, silver, black and blue
home arena: Pepsi Center
Stanley Cups won: 2

EDMONTON OILERS
team colors: white, navy blue, orange and red
home arena: Rexall Place
Stanley Cups won: 5

MINNESOTA WILD
team colors: red, green, gold and wheat
home arena: Xcel Energy Center

VANCOUVER CANUCKS
team colors: blue, silver, red and white
home arena: General Motors Place
mascot: Fin

PACIFIC DIVISION

ANAHEIM DUCKS
nickname: Ducks
team colors: purple, green, silver and white
home arena: Honda Center
mascot: Wild Wing
Stanley Cups won: 1

DALLAS STARS
team colors: green, white, black and gold
home arena: American Airlines Center
Stanley Cups won: 1

LOS ANGELES KINGS
team colors: purple, white, black and silver
home arena: STAPLES Center

PHOENIX COYOTES
team colors: red, green, sand, sienna and purple
home arena: Jobing.com Arena
mascot: Howler

SAN JOSE SHARKS
team colors: teal, gray, orange and black
home arena: HP Pavilion
mascot: S.J. Sharkie

WESTERN CONFERENCE

YOUR FAVORITE TEAM

Name of your favorite team: _____

Conference and division: _____

Players on your favorite team at the start of the season:

Number	Name	Position
_____	_____	_____
_____	_____	_____
_____	_____	_____
_____	_____	_____
_____	_____	_____
_____	_____	_____
_____	_____	_____
_____	_____	_____
_____	_____	_____
_____	_____	_____
_____	_____	_____
_____	_____	_____
_____	_____	_____

Changes, Trades, New Players

_____ _____ _____
_____ _____ _____
_____ _____ _____
_____ _____ _____
_____ _____ _____
_____ _____ _____
_____ _____ _____
_____ _____ _____

End-of-Season Standings

Fill in the name of the team you think will finish in first place in each of the six NHL Divisions.

EASTERN CONFERENCE

ATLANTIC DIVISION

NORTHEAST DIVISION

SOUTHEAST DIVISION

_____

_____

_____

CENTRAL DIVISION

NORTHWEST DIVISION

PACIFIC DIVISION

WESTERN CONFERENCE

_____

_____

_____

The Playoffs

Which two teams will meet in the Stanley Cup Final? Fill in their names below, then circle the team you think will win.

Eastern Conference Winner: _____

Western Conference Winner: _____

YOUR FAVORITE TEAM

Your Team — All Season Long

The standings of hockey teams are listed on the sports pages of the newspaper all season long. The standings will show you which team is in first place, second place, etc., right down to last place.

Some of the abbreviations you'll become familiar with are: GP for games played; W for wins; L for losses; OT for overtime losses; PTS for points; A for assists; G for goals.

Check the standings on the same day of every month and copy down what they say about your team. By keeping track of your team this way you'll be able to see when it was playing well and when it wasn't.

	GP	W	L	OT	PTS
NOVEMBER 1					
DECEMBER 1					
JANUARY 1					
FEBRUARY 1					
MARCH 1					
APRIL 1					
MAY 1					

Final Standings

At the end of the season print the final record of your team below.

YOUR TEAM	GP	W	L	OT	PTS

Your Favorite Players' Scoring Records

While you're keeping track of your favorite team during the season, you can also follow the progress of your favorite players. Just fill in their point totals on the same day of every month.

player	nov 1	dec 1	jan 1	feb 1	mar 1	apr 1	may 1

Your Favorite Goaltenders' Records

You can keep track of your favorite goaltenders' averages during the season. Just fill in the information below.

GAA is the abbreviation for goals-against average. That's the average number of goals given up by a goaltender during a game over the course of the season.

player	nov 1	dec 1	jan 1	feb 1	mar 1	apr 1	may 1

As a hockey fan, chances are you were in front of a television on February 28, 2010, watching the Olympic gold-medal hockey game between Canada and the U.S. But did you know that the man who scored and won the gold for Canada — creating the "where were you?" moment for millions of Canadians — didn't even see the puck go in?

"I just shot it, and then I saw everyone stand up, and I heard the horn and everything," said Sidney after the game. "It's a pretty amazing feeling. You're pretty excited, but you just try to take it in because that's what you dream of doing."

> **"Great players do great things, and Sid hadn't scored in a couple of games. But they [great players] just seem to find a way."**
> **— Team Canada coach Mike Babcock, after the gold-medal game**

There has been no shortage of dreams coming true for "Sid the Kid." Drafted first overall in 2005 and expected to lead the rebirth of the Pittsburgh Penguins, Sidney has taken on the challenge with a tremendous work ethic and determination to win. He became one of the youngest captains in NHL history, won the NHL scoring title, won the Hart Memorial Trophy as the NHL's Most Valuable Player and, in 2009, helped Pittsburgh win the Stanley Cup. Add to all of that the Olympic "Golden Goal" and you have enough dreams to satisfy a

dozen careers, never mind just one.

"Sid really cemented himself in Canadian hockey history," said Pittsburgh teammate Bill Guerin. "Nobody's ever going to forget that goal he scored."

Does the goal rank up there with the all-time greatest goals in the history of hockey? It's difficult to say. Every generation of fans has its own memorable moments.

"For a seven- or eight-year-old kid, this will be the one where he'll say he watched the game with his parents and 'I know where I was at that time' and, that way, it's pretty cool," says Sid.

It's exciting for hockey fans to consider that Sidney has been a part of so many big moments but hasn't even turned 24 yet. His best years as a player are still ahead of him. How cool is that?

HOCKEY MEMORY

Will Sid ever top scoring the gold medal — winning goal for Canada in the Olympics, in overtime, in Canada? "Dreams are dreams and you never know if they're going to come true, but that one did," says Sid.

DID YOU KNOW?

Everyone knows that 87 is an important number for Sid, marking the year and even the month and day of his birth. But he also signed a contract extension in 2007 that pays him an average of $8.7 million per year.

2009–2010 STATS

GP	G	A	PTS	PIM
81	51	58	109	71

Pittsburgh Penguins' 1st choice, 1st overall, in the 2005 NHL Entry Draft
1st NHL Team, Season: Pittsburgh Penguins, 2005–2006
Born: August 7, 1987, in Cole Harbour, Nova Scotia
Position: Center
Shoots: Left
Height: 1.80 m (5'11")
Weight: 91 kg (200 lbs.)

Drew Doughty was drafted by the LA Kings as the second overall pick in 2008. One of the reasons he was rated so highly was because most scouts agreed he had the skills to be able to step right into the NHL. Many players, even high picks, often need an extra season in junior hockey, or a season or two in the minors, so that they can polish their game. Drew wasn't one of those guys. He played in 81 games for the Kings, led the team in ice time, and was named to the 2009 All-Rookie Team. In his second season, Drew continued to push ahead, developing his game further and becoming one of the top defensemen in the league.

"Growing up it was my dream to make the NHL, but you never think it's going to come true. You want it to happen, but you know how tough it is."

"I think with him, he just gets the game," said one of his defensive partners, veteran Sean O'Donnell. "He understands it, he's got great anticipation and he loves to compete."

Like any rookie, Drew had a few jittery nights during his first season. After all, he was playing in the best league in the world at the age of only 18. But as the season went on, he looked more and more comfortable. Last season he had the poise of someone who'd been in the league for half a dozen years, not just one.

"I remember in my first game, I was in awe at times of how fast the game was, and I just got lost out there," recalls Drew with a smile.

Drew's skills earned him a spot on Canada's Olympic hockey team last February. He started as the seventh defenseman but, by the second period of the opening game, he was taking a regular shift. He was even on the ice when Sidney Crosby scored the winning goal in overtime.

After the Olympics, it was back to Los Angeles for the rest of the regular season, followed by his first taste of NHL playoff action. Drew has done more in two seasons than a lot of players manage in an entire career. And it's likely to get better.

HOCKEY MEMORY
Despite growing up a long way from Los Angeles, in London, Ontario, Drew was a Kings fan. "They had Gretzky, so they were pretty good."

DID YOU KNOW?
As a 20-year-old at the Olympics, Drew was the youngest player to represent Canada at a major international tournament since Eric Lindros played in the 1991 Canada Cup.

2009–2010 STATS

GP	G	A	PTS	PIM
82	16	43	59	54

Los Angeles Kings' 1st choice, 2nd overall, in the 2008 NHL Entry Draft
1st NHL Team, Season: Los Angeles Kings, 2008–2009
Born: December 8, 1989, in London, Ontario
Position: Defense
Shoots: Right
Height: 1.85 m (6'1")
Weight: 92 kg (203 lbs.)

MIKE FISHER

Mike Fisher is the kind of player most coaches and teammates love. He may never put up the type of numbers that his teammate Daniel Alfredsson does, but he's just as important to the team. Mike is a great competitor who will give his all night after night.

"Mike's a great, great guy that's respected within the room," says Ottawa captain Alfredsson. "He brings a lot of character, and he's definitely one of the best team-guys you can have."

> "He works extremely hard in the areas that some guys don't like to go to: in front of the net, in the corners . . . he'll block shots. He does a lot of little things well."
> — Ottawa coach Cory Clouston

Mike has had to fight through his fair share of adversity during his 10 seasons with the Sens. His rookie season (1999–2000) was pretty much a write-off after he injured his knee early in the season during a game against the Boston Bruins. Mike needed major reconstructive surgery on the knee, so he missed the rest of the season. Then, in October 2003, Mike hurt his elbow and had to have surgery, missing most of that season as well. But through it all, he's battled hard. The last three seasons he's missed only 10 games. Mike also had his career-best scoring season last year with 25 goals and 28 assists for 53 points — third-best on the team.

That was quite a turnaround from 2008–2009 when he managed only 32 points in 78 games.

"The coach has given me a more offensive role than last year," said Mike early last season. "I just felt like the puck was going my way and I was getting more bounces."

There were times last season when Mike had to shoulder a little more of the offensive load for the club than he normally would have, specifically when the top two scorers, Alfredsson and Jason Spezza, were both injured at the same time. Although Fisher was never going to be able to duplicate the offense the Sens would normally have gotten from Alfie or Spezza, he pressed hard and tried to lead by example. That's what he's done his entire career.

HOCKEY MEMORY
Mike is from the hockey hotbed of Peterborough, Ontario, and remembers watching future NHLers like Mike Ricci, Tie Domi and Chris Pronger.

DID YOU KNOW?
When he gets the chance, Mike absolutely loves to hunt and fish. He finds it relaxing and a great way to unwind. Mike has been grizzly bear hunting in Alaska and once caught a 100-pound marlin on a deep-sea fishing expedition to Mexico and the Cayman Islands.

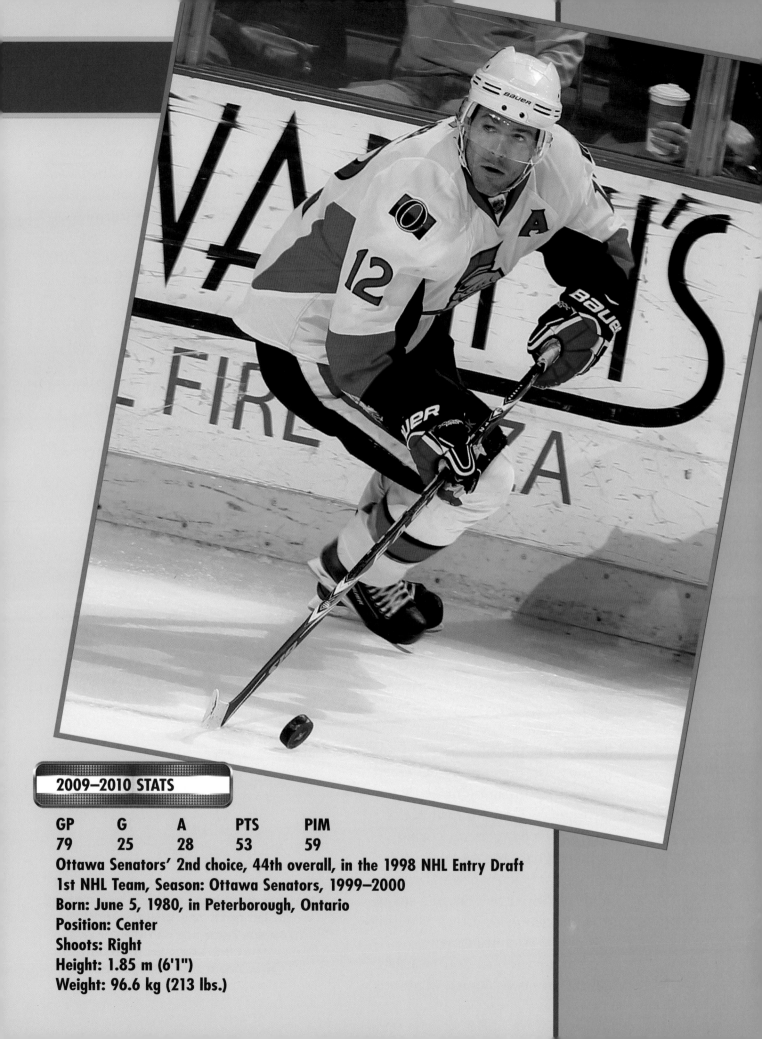

2009–2010 STATS

GP	G	A	PTS	PIM
79	25	28	53	59

Ottawa Senators' 2nd choice, 44th overall, in the 1998 NHL Entry Draft
1st NHL Team, Season: Ottawa Senators, 1999–2000
Born: June 5, 1980, in Peterborough, Ontario
Position: Center
Shoots: Right
Height: 1.85 m (6'1")
Weight: 96.6 kg (213 lbs.)

MARIAN GABORIK

It was strange to see Marian Gaborik in the red, white and blue of the New York Rangers last season. Before he signed a five-year deal as an unrestricted free agent with the "Broadway Blueshirts," Marian had played his entire NHL career with the Minnesota Wild. He was the Wild's first ever draft pick, and he left the club as the all-time franchise scoring leader. The Rangers surprised many by paying big bucks for Marian — $37.5 million over five years. After all, he had battled injuries in 2008–2009, leaving him to play only 17 games. But Rangers' team doctors gave Marian a clean bill of health.

> "When I'm going down the ice, and I'm open and I get the puck, it's the best feeling. When you just have the goalie in front of you, you've just got to put it in, right?"

The Rangers expected that Marian could add some punch to their offense. The team's inability to score had been a problem for them in the playoffs the previous spring. Marian certainly delivered last season, finishing up with his highest offensive total ever, leading the Rangers in scoring with 42 goals and 44 assists for 86 points. One man who wasn't at all surprised by Marian's strong season was his long-time coach in Minnesota, Jacques Lemaire.

It's interesting to hear Lemaire talk about how talented Marian is as a scorer. Lemaire had a well-earned reputation as one of the top defensive coaches in the game, and he often clashed with his star player in Minnesota because he wanted more out of Marian defensively. But whether Marian is driving toward the net to score or hustling back to help out defensively, it's his speed that separates him from the rest of the pack.

"I love speed, and I think it's my number one weapon on the ice," says Marian.

So far, Rangers fans would agree. Marian has given the Blueshirts more speed and made them more of an offensive threat. That's exactly what they had hoped for.

HOCKEY MEMORY
Marian has a memory that only a few players share: in the history of the NHL, a player has scored five or more goals in a regular season game only 54 times. Marian's five-goal effort against the New York Rangers on December 20, 2007, is the most recent addition to the very short list.

DID YOU KNOW?
Marian's love of speed extends off the ice. He loves to race go-karts when he gets the chance, and he also has a race car simulator in his house that he uses to sharpen his hand-eye co-ordination.

2009–2010 STATS

GP	G	A	PTS	PIM
76	42	44	86	37

Minnesota Wild's 1st choice, 3rd overall, in the 2000 NHL Entry Draft
1st NHL Team, Season: Minnesota Wild, 2000–2001
Born: February 14, 1982, in Trencin, Czechoslovakia (now Slovakia)
Position: Right Wing
Shoots: Left
Height: 1.85 m (6'1")
Weight: 90 kg (199 lbs.)

JAROSLAV HALAK

Last season, Montreal coach Jacques Martin had two number-one goalies in his lineup. This meant he was in the difficult position of having to give two very good goalies enough playing time to keep each of them happy.

Jaroslav Halak played only four more games than Carey Price last season, but in the minds of most, Jaroslav was the clear number-one. He won more games and had a better goals-against-average than Price. By the end of the season, and into the playoffs, Jaro started in most of the big games. But Jaro wasn't bothered with who was number one.

"The thing is, we both want to play, of course. It is the team that needs to win, whether it is me or him."

"I think he's proven what he can do all season long and the Olympics just sealed it for him. I definitely believe he has what it takes to be a number-one goalie in this league."
— Slovakian Olympic teammate Andrej Meszaros

Jaroslav was a very late pick in the 2003 NHL Entry Draft (271st overall). He didn't play his first game for the Habs until 2006–2007, and then he started the following season in the minors. It was a frustrating time.

It all seemed to come together last season, though. He played in a career-high 45 games, finishing with 26 wins, 13 losses, 5 overtime losses and a 2.40 goals-against average. And then there was the Winter Olympics: Jaro played every minute of every game for Slovakia and helped to lead the team to a fourth place finish, their highest finish ever at the Olympic Games. And then there was his amazing performance in the playoffs, as he led Montreal to upsets against Washington and Pittsburgh.

However, in a surprise move, Jaroslav was traded by the Habs to the St. Louis Blues in early June. Montreal knew they had two potential number one goalies, but could only afford one.

"When I got the news, obviously I was surprised," says Jaroslav. "I'll try to make the new organization proud they got me."

If he can continue to play the way he did in last year's playoffs, that won't be too hard.

HOCKEY MEMORY

As a young boy, Jaro loved to collect hockey cards, particularly goalies'. His most prized card was the first Patrick Roy card issued after he was traded from Montreal to Colorado.

DID YOU KNOW?

Halak had a special mask that he wore for Slovakia during the Olympics. On one side, there was a painted portrait of Vladimir Dzurilla — the greatest Slovak goalie. On the other side was a picture of Slovak folk hero Juraj Janosik.

2009–2010 STATS

GP	W	L	OT	GAA	SO
45	26	13	5	2.40	5

Montreal Canadiens' 11th choice, 271st overall, in the 2003 NHL Entry Draft
1st NHL Team, Season: Montreal Canadiens, 2006–2007
Born: May 13, 1985, in Bratislava, Czechoslovakia (now Slovakia)
Position: Goaltender
Catches: Left
Height: 1.80 m (5'11")
Weight: 83 kg (182 lbs.)

JAROME IGINLA

Jarome Iginla has done his job, there's no doubt about that. He led the Calgary Flames in scoring once again last season, topping the 30-goal mark for the ninth season in a row. But Jarome and the rest of the team are still trying to find happiness in the NHL playoffs. As the team's captain, Jarome wants to lead his team to the ultimate prize — the Stanley Cup.

"It's the hardest trophy to win in professional sports," he says. "You play all year, and it's so tight. There's really no rest for the whole season. Then you get to the playoffs, and you have another two or three months to go of gruelling, physical battles."

"Part of being captain is understanding it's definitely not one guy. It's important to have help in assistants and older guys that have been around."

The Flames haven't been so lucky in terms of lasting those two or three months. Since their run to the Final in 2004, they've either missed the playoffs or gone out in the first round every season.

But 2009–2010 was a strange season for Jarome. While the Flames missed the playoffs, he will no doubt look back on a year that saw him assist on one of the biggest goals in Canadian hockey history: Sidney Crosby's gold-medal winner in overtime against the U.S. at the Winter Olympics. It was Jarome who dug the puck from

along the boards and made the pass to Crosby, who was yelling for the puck.

"There's different pitches of yelling," says Iginla, smiling. "He was yelling [for the puck] pretty urgently."

Jarome had fallen to the ice after making the pass, so he didn't actually see the winner. But he heard the roar of the crowd.

"I couldn't believe it. It was done. I didn't see where he put it or anything, I just saw him jumping around. It was amazing."

That "amazing" feeling is something Jarome would love to experience in a Calgary sweater as a Stanley Cup champion, and, judging by past performance, you know Jarome will do everything he can to make that happen.

HOCKEY MEMORY

Jarome fondly recalls his days in junior hockey with the Kamloops Blazers in the Western Hockey League. He scored 246 points in three seasons with the Blazers and was a part of two Memorial Cup Championships.

DID YOU KNOW?

While at the 2002 Winter Olympics in Salt Lake City, Jarome was talking to a few young men from Calgary who were at the Games, but sleeping in their car. Next thing they knew, Jarome had booked them a room in a hotel and paid for it.

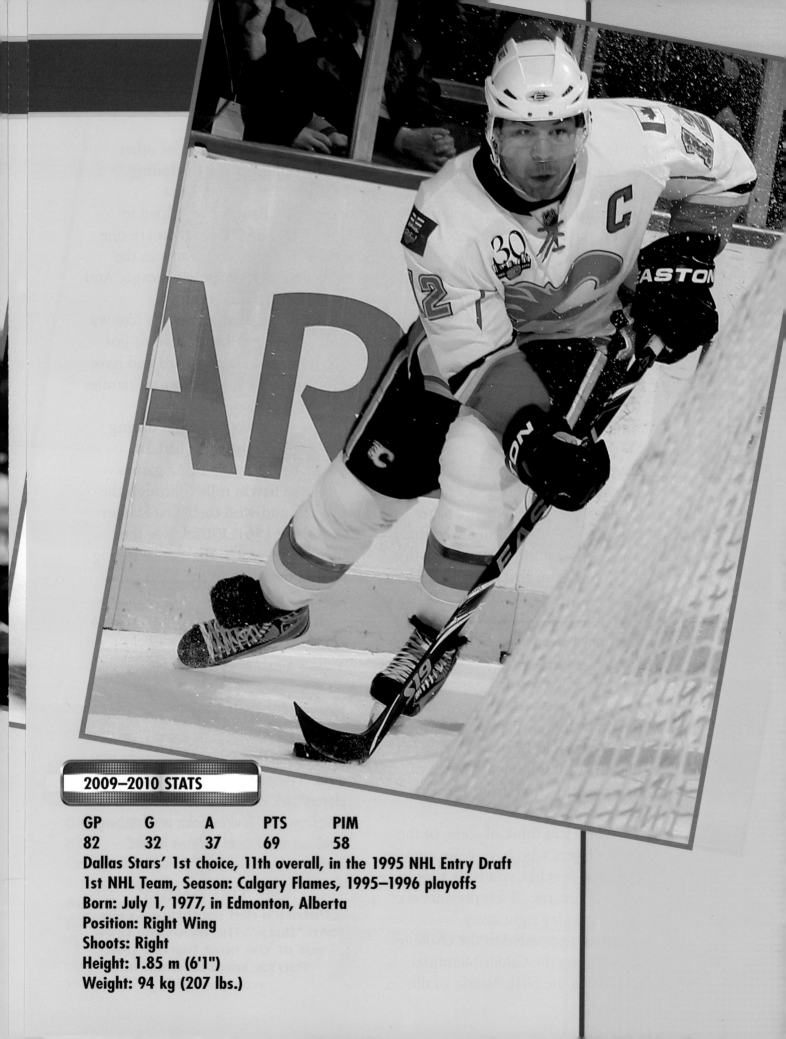

2009–2010 STATS

GP	G	A	PTS	PIM
82	32	37	69	58

Dallas Stars' 1st choice, 11th overall, in the 1995 NHL Entry Draft
1st NHL Team, Season: Calgary Flames, 1995–1996 playoffs
Born: July 1, 1977, in Edmonton, Alberta
Position: Right Wing
Shoots: Right
Height: 1.85 m (6'1")
Weight: 94 kg (207 lbs.)

EVGENI MALKIN

Evgeni Malkin has grown a lot in the last four years. Not just physically, but as a hockey player. When he arrived in Pittsburgh in 2006, he could barely speak a word of English and was faced with the incredible challenge of becoming a top player in the best hockey league in the world. Four seasons later, he's sipped champagne from the Stanley Cup, won three different awards (Calder Memorial Trophy, Art Ross Trophy and Conn Smythe Trophy) and become one of the greatest players in the NHL. On top of all that, he's also learned to speak English and feels right at home in his adopted country, the United States. That's a lot of progress to make in a pretty short period.

> **"I think he's found out how much of a presence and how dominant he can be out there."**
> **— Sidney Crosby**

"I think he's adjusted well to the new lifestyle," says teammate and fellow Russian Sergei Gonchar, who had to make the same kinds of adjustments when he broke into the NHL over 15 years ago. "Now that he's comfortable here, it helps him on the ice, and he's a better player for it."

Malkin is intelligent, and he's learned quickly, both in terms of hockey and adapting to a new culture away from the rink. He gives a lot of credit to the veteran, Gonchar.

"I think what Sergei did for me, it's hard to put a price on it. What he did for me, I think I will be forever in debt to him," says Evgeni. "Every day we talked and he'd explain everything to me . . . Sergei became like an older brother to me."

Evgeni missed a few games last season with shoulder and ankle injuries, which is why he finished with the lowest point total of his career. However, he still averaged well over a point per game. And chances are, if he stays healthy this season, "Geno" will be right back on top of the scoring parade. Although the Pens were defeated by the Montreal Canadiens in a dramatic seven-game series in last year's playoffs, Pittsburgh fans can expect another exciting season with both Crosby and Malkin in the lineup.

HOCKEY MEMORY

Evgeni remembers spending time with his father and brother on an ice rink. "When we were young, we were always there day and night and then we got old enough to play as part of an [organized] team."

DID YOU KNOW?

One of Evgeni's favorite meals is borscht, a traditional Russian and Ukrainian soup made from potatoes and beets. His mother, Natalia, makes it for him whenever she's in town.

GP	G	A	PTS	PIM
67	28	49	77	100

Pittsburgh Penguins' 1st choice, 2nd overall, in the 2004 NHL Entry Draft
1st NHL Team, Season: Pittsburgh Penguins, 2006–2007
Born: July 31, 1986, in Magnitogorsk, Russia
Position: Center
Shoots: Left
Height: 1.92 m (6'3")
Weight: 88 kg (195 lbs.)

SAN JOSE SHARKS

Last season didn't start off so well for San Jose's Patrick Marleau. After wearing the C as Sharks' team captain for four seasons, the club's management decided to make a switch and give it to veteran defenseman Rob Blake. Coach Todd McLellan said that the move wasn't a reflection on Patrick's leadership.

How Patrick responded to the situation said more about his leadership ability than any letter stitched onto his sweater ever could.

"I'm still going to lead whether I have something on my sweater or not," said Patrick. "That part doesn't change . . . I still look at myself as a leader of this team."

> "It feels good. If anything, you want to set the bar as high as you can and try to move up there."
> — Patrick, on his career best 44-goal season

As if to prove it, Patrick recorded a career high nine-game point-scoring streak less than a month into the season. He finished up with a career high of 44 goals and added 39 assists for 83 points, the second-highest points total of his career. He was named the club's MVP for the second year in a row and the third time in his career.

"He's done exactly what everyone wanted him to do, from day one right through," said Blake.

It was a season of milestones for Patrick: he played in his 900th career game (all of them with San Jose), racked up his 300th NHL goal and also helped Canada win a gold medal at the Winter Olympics.

"That 300 goals is quite an accomplishment," said teammate Joe Thornton. "He's played great his whole career with this team. I can't say enough about Patty."

C or no C, as he suits up for his 13th season with the Sharks, Patrick will once again be one of the leaders on a very talented team.

HOCKEY MEMORY

Patrick will never forget the feeling of winning a gold medal at home at the 2010 Winter Olympics when Canada defeated the USA in overtime. "It was complete pandemonium. The whole experience really reminded you of where you come from."

DID YOU KNOW?

Early in his career with the Sharks, Patrick wore the number 14 because "it was pretty much the only one left when I got here." He switched to his preferred number 12 once it became available.

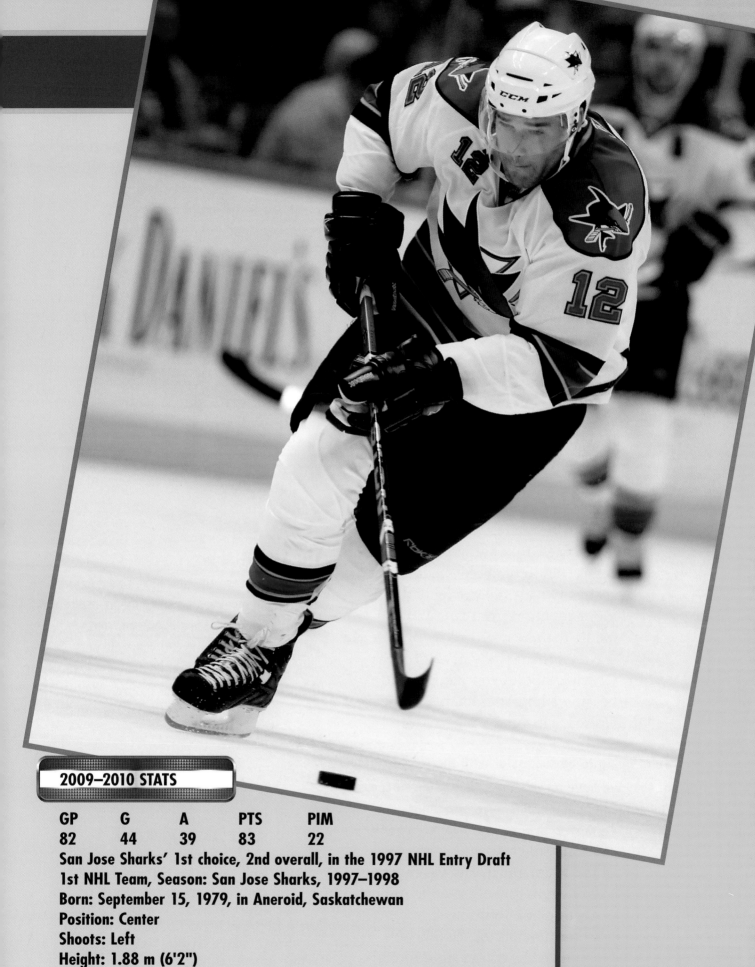

2009–2010 STATS

GP	G	A	PTS	PIM
82	44	39	83	22

San Jose Sharks' 1st choice, 2nd overall, in the 1997 NHL Entry Draft
1st NHL Team, Season: San Jose Sharks, 1997–1998
Born: September 15, 1979, in Aneroid, Saskatchewan
Position: Center
Shoots: Left
Height: 1.88 m (6'2")
Weight: 99.8 kg (220 lbs.)

Buffalo Sabres fans have known for a few seasons how special Ryan Miller is: he's been the Sabres' number one goalie since 2005–2006. Miller was even recognized as a great goalie back in his college hockey days at Michigan State University: he was named the CCHA Player of the Year twice and won the Hobey Baker Award as the top U.S. collegiate player in 2001. But it was during the Olympic Games last February that Ryan became known to hockey fans around the world.

The Olympics are a big deal for many reasons, but one of them is that almost every sports fan in the world watches them. So when Ryan's stellar play in goal took Team USA to the gold-medal game against Canada, he suddenly drew more attention from fans and media than he ever had before. He was even named the MVP of the Olympic hockey tournament and became a household name in the United States and Canada.

"If we're going to be successful with the world-class talent that we have on this team, it's going to come from attitude and willingness to compete."

"Ryan Miller was the best goalie of the tournament. He was our best player every game," said Olympic teammate Erik Johnson.

Miller flew out of the red-hot Olympic competition right into the white heat of an NHL stretch drive and then the playoffs with the Sabres. Buffalo finished with 100 points and Ryan recorded career bests with 41 wins and a 2.22 goals-against-average.

The Sabres ran into a determined Boston Bruins team in the first round of the playoffs. It didn't help that three of Buffalo's top six forwards were either out of the lineup or playing injured. In the end, the Bruins knocked the Sabres out in six hard-fought games. Buffalo will be looking for a repeat of their regular season success this year. Another big season from Ryan will go a long way in helping them achieve their goals.

HOCKEY MEMORY

On playing in the Olympic gold-medal game and coming away with a silver medal after losing to Canada: "I'm still going to wake up when I'm 60, 80 or 100 years old and wish we'd won a gold, but I'm going to keep things in perspective. It was positive. We had fun. We had a great group of guys and that's what's important."

DID YOU KNOW?

Ryan is an avid photographer. He first became interested in the hobby during his days at Michigan State. "It's peaceful, it's laid-back and it's on my own time," says Ryan. "It's a little like goaltending where you can just kind of do your own thing."

2009–2010 STATS

GP	W	L	OT	GAA	SO
69	41	18	8	2.22	5

Buffalo Sabres' 7th choice, 138th overall, in the 1999 NHL Entry Draft
1st NHL Team, Season: Buffalo Sabres, 2002–2003
Born: July 17, 1980, in East Lansing, Michigan
Position: Goaltender
Catches: Left
Height: 1.88 m (6'2")
Weight: 77 kg (170 lbs.)

ALEX OVECHKIN

Alex first picked up a hockey stick when he was just two years old. Not surprisingly, it was tough to get him to put it down. Alex's father was athletic and his mother Tatiana was one of the best female basketball players in the world, winning two Olympic gold medals with the Soviet Union. So it isn't surprising that Alex's parents encouraged him to work hard to try to become a good hockey player. But they also insisted that he have fun while doing it. And that's the kind of attitude Alex has kept during his career. Maybe that's one of the reasons he always seems to be smiling.

"I don't feel pressure when I play. I feel like I have freedom," says Alex. "I just have fun. I love it."

"I knew it would be hard to come to the NHL. I didn't know the league and I didn't know anybody. But I just tell myself that you have to be yourself and play how you can."

When Alex was drafted first overall by Washington in 2004, Caps fans were told that he was the player who was going to lead the team from being mediocre to a Stanley Cup contender. It's difficult to know if that pressure has ever bothered Alex. If it has, he's certainly never said so.

"It's hard to play in the NHL, and it's hard to try to be the best, but I love it. Even when you're in a different arena and people boo you sometimes. It's all fun."

Up until the time Alex was a small boy, Russian players weren't allowed to play in other countries. But Alex grew up during a time when things were changing and many of the best players were being allowed to leave the Russian league and go to North America to play in the NHL. As a boy, Alex saw great Russian league players like Sergei Fedorov, Pavel Bure and Alexei Zhamnov leave and go on to become stars in the NHL.

"I was a little kid at the time, but it was huge," recalls Alex. "I think it's good for little kids to be able to see that they can go and play somewhere else like the NHL."

There is no doubt that Alex is inspiring the next generation of great Russian players.

HOCKEY MEMORY
After Russia defeated Canada in the gold-medal game at the 2008 World Hockey Championship in Quebec City, Alex dug the Canadian team's "Lucky Loonie" out of the ice and had a necklace made with half of the coin (a teammate took the other half).

DID YOU KNOW?
Alex is one of the few big name players in the sports world who doesn't use an agent to negotiate his contract with his team. Instead, Alex consults with his mother, father and other trusted family members.

2009–2010 STATS

GP	G	A	PTS	PIM
72	50	59	109	89

Washington Capitals' 1st choice, 1st overall, in the 2004 NHL Entry Draft
1st NHL Team, Season: Washington Capitals, 2005–2006
Born: September 17, 1985, in Moscow, USSR (now Russia)
Position: Left Wing
Shoots: Right
Height: 1.88 m (6'2")
Weight: 100 kg (220 lbs.)

ZACH PARISE

NEW JERSEY DEVILS

Zach Parise can remember watching the 1994 Winter Olympics when he was 10 years old and seeing Peter Forsberg's dramatic goal against Canada that won Sweden the gold medal in a shootout. Sixteen years later, Zach found himself wearing the red, white and blue of the United States and playing in the 2010 Olympic gold-medal game against Canada. As it turned out, Zach scored a dramatic goal of his own. He tied the game 2–2 with only 25 seconds remaining in regulation time. Unfortunately for Zach and his U.S. teammates, they lost to Canada 3–2 in overtime. It was a bitter defeat for Zach to handle.

"I love that feeling of scoring goals. It's just, you work so hard in the off-season, you work so hard growing up and then when you finally make it . . . when you score a goal there's no better feeling for me."

"Being so close and then losing in overtime . . . I thought we played great the whole tournament and got better every game. It's tough to take when you were that close to winning," said Zach after the game.

Zach knew what a great experience the Olympics had been. But he also knew that it would have to be back to regular business right away: the Devils were in a tough race with Pittsburgh for first place in the Atlantic Division. In the end, the Devils led their division and were second in the Eastern Conference with 103 points. Zach led the Devils in scoring (38 goals, 44 assists, 82 points) and was named the Devils' Most Valuable Player for the second season in a row. He became the first New Jersey player to record four straight 30-goal seasons.

"He's a guy that seems to always find a way to get it done with his desire, game in and game out," says former Devils MVP and Hall of Famer Scott Stevens.

New Jersey's strong regular season play seemed to dry up in the playoffs as they were upset in the first round by Philadelphia. Perhaps without the Olympics to worry about this season, Zach and his teammates may have a little more left to give come playoff time. Zach's expectations certainly won't change much: score the big goals and help the team succeed.

HOCKEY MEMORY

Zach's earliest hockey memories are all about growing up in Bloomington, Minnesota, and watching and playing the game with his older brother, Jordan. "Bloomington is a great hockey place. A lot of good players came out of there."

DID YOU KNOW?

Zach is a pretty good tennis player, and has been known to pair up with teammate Travis Zajac for doubles matches against some of the other Devils players.

2009–2010 STATS

GP	G	A	PTS	PIM
81	38	44	82	32

New Jersey Devils' 1st choice, 17th overall, in the 2003 NHL Entry Draft
1st NHL Team, Season: New Jersey Devils, 2005–2006
Born: July 28, 1984, in Minneapolis, Minnesota
Position: Left Wing
Shoots: Left
Height: 1.80 m (5'11")
Weight: 86 kg (190 lbs.)

BRAD RICHARDS

DALLAS STARS

When Brad Richards was traded to the Dallas Stars in a deadline deal on February 26, 2008, it was supposed to be the start of a new chapter in his great career. Before the deal, Brad had played every game of his NHL career for Tampa Bay. He had hoisted the Stanley Cup, and was named the Conn Smythe Trophy winner as the playoffs' Most Valuable Player in 2004. He liked his teammates and the city. But still, Brad was ready to turn the page, and welcomed the chance to play in Dallas.

Brad joined his new team, was part of a good run and even made it to the semi-finals. But then came his first full season with the Stars. Brad played in only 56 games — missing 25 of the team's last 26 games with injuries to his back, wrist and hand. It was a nightmare, but Brad was determined that he would be in top shape heading into last season.

"As a player, you always look at every team like it's a big battle . . . Every game is a dogfight now. It's a tough league."

"I took the opportunity to try to get everything cleared up and be one hundred percent heading into training camp," said Brad.

Brad's hard work paid off. He got off to a great start, picking up points in 13 of the first 15 games he played. He ended up leading the Stars in scoring, finishing with 24 goals, 67 assists and 91 points — a point total equaling his career best from 2005–2006.

My first year here, with all the injuries, is something I'd rather just forget," says Brad. "It feels more like home now. I love what Joe Nieuwendyk [general manager] and Marc Crawford [head coach] have brought. It's working really well."

Like most NHL teams, the Stars are a work in progress. It's tough to be successful in the best hockey league in the world. But a veteran like Brad can certainly help things along. His experience, in tough situations and big games, make him a big part of the Dallas Stars' plans for the next few seasons. Those plans include another trip to the Stanley Cup final for Brad.

HOCKEY MEMORY

According to Brad, his greatest hockey memories so far are "playing my first NHL game [against the NY Islanders in 2000] and winning the Cup in 2004 with the Lightning."

DID YOU KNOW?

Brad is a bit of a wine connoisseur. After the Lightning won the Stanley Cup in 2004, Brad and some of his teammates took the Cup to a local restaurant and sampled some classic, old wines using the Cup as a giant wine glass.

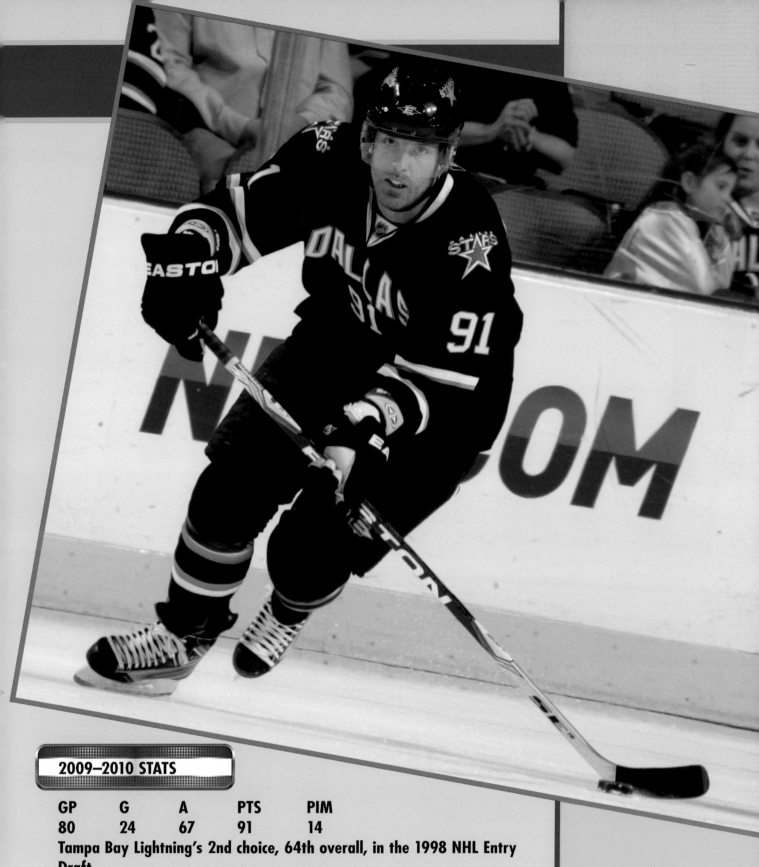

2009–2010 STATS

GP	G	A	PTS	PIM
80	24	67	91	14

Tampa Bay Lightning's 2nd choice, 64th overall, in the 1998 NHL Entry
Draft

1st NHL Team, Season: Tampa Bay Lightning, 2000–2001

Born: May 2, 1980, in Murray Harbour, Prince Edward Island

Position: Center

Shoots: Left

Height: 1.83 m (6')

Weight: 87 kg (192 lbs.)

Henrik Sedin

It isn't as though hockey fans ever doubted Henrik Sedin's ability. Henrik handles the puck beautifully, can read the play like few others and has a very good shot. But Canucks fans were still a little surprised when Henrik, after nine seasons, suddenly started to put up points at the same pace as the game's greatest. He battled Alex Ovechkin and Sidney Crosby for the NHL scoring title, before winning it with a career best 112 points. Had he changed his game?

According to some, the secret was that Henrik was shooting more and passing less. His usual linemate, twin brother Daniel Sedin, was usually the goal-scorer on the line, with Henrik playing more the role of set-up man. But Daniel went down for 18 games with a foot injury early in the season and, all of a sudden, it was Henrik who had to take on the role of finisher.

> **"It's confidence, and you get confidence from hard work and knowing you're prepared. If you're well prepared, you're going to do a good job and you're going to be confident."**

"I think the Daniel injury just kind of forced him into being more of a shooter," said Vancouver assistant coach Rick Bowness. "I think the two of them were just so used to looking for each other with one guy being the finisher and the other guy the set-up guy. But when the finisher isn't there, the set-up guy has to shoot."

Once Daniel returned to the lineup, Henrik just kept on doing what he was doing. The line (of the two Sedins and Alex Burrows) was good to start with, but then hit an even higher level as Henrik continued to chase the NHL scoring title.

Henrik's biggest fan, Daniel, could see the change in his brother's game. He thought it came down to confidence.

"He holds on to the puck for that extra second or two to get guys open. It's fun to see, and it's fun to play with him."

Henrik Sedin is proof that no matter how long you've played the game, you can always get better.

Hockey Memory

Henrik's Art Ross Trophy win last season as the NHL's top scorer is a memory he'll have forever. He became only the second Swedish-born player ever to win the scoring title (Peter Forsberg, in 2003, was the other).

Did You Know?

Henrik and Daniel's contracts both expired after the 2008–09 season, and Canucks fans didn't think the team would be able to afford to keep both players under the salary cap. But the twins both said they would only sign with a team if they could stay together. They ended up taking a small drop in salary so they could both remain in Vancouver, a city they love.

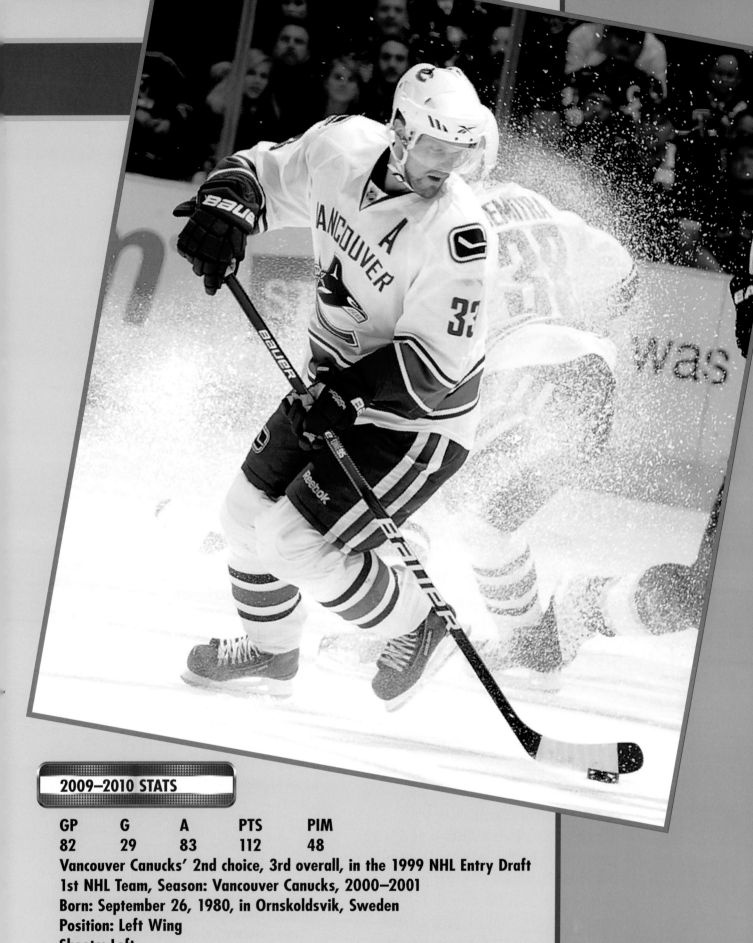

GP	G	A	PTS	PIM
82	29	83	112	48

Vancouver Canucks' 2nd choice, 3rd overall, in the 1999 NHL Entry Draft
1st NHL Team, Season: Vancouver Canucks, 2000–2001
Born: September 26, 1980, in Ornskoldsvik, Sweden
Position: Left Wing
Shoots: Left
Height: 1.85 m (6'1")
Weight: 84 kg (185 lbs.)

JOE THORNTON

Joe Thornton's career stats paint a picture of a player who can put up points. Heading into this season, Joe has a total of 931 career points in 12 seasons — that's an average of over one point per game. But if you look at Thornton's numbers a little more closely, what becomes clear is that he really makes his mark as a playmaker rather than a goal-scorer. Joe has only topped the 30-goal mark twice in his entire career. That's a remarkably low total for a player who's among the top active point scorers. But his sky-high assist totals makes up for his low goal totals: he has led the NHL in assists four of the last six seasons. Last season, Joe led his team and finished second in the league with 69 assists.

> **"My focus coming to the rink is always to work as hard as I can."**

Of course, the people who benefit from Thornton's great playmaking skills are his linemates. Patrick Marleau, who has spent most of the last two seasons playing on a line with Joe, has enjoyed the two best seasons of his career. Dany Heatley spent much of last season playing on a line with Joe and was impressed by his teammate's skill.

"There are a lot of great passers in this league, but his size and strength set him apart," says Heatley. "He can hold guys off for twenty, thirty seconds to make the play."

Something else Joe brings to the rink with the Sharks is his leadership. He's been around the league long enough to how important it is that a team have strong guidance on and off the ice. Sometimes that means calling a teammate out. But it's all part of growing as a team.

"I think [if players have words] it just shows that we care for one another, actually," says Joe. "You have to push each other and know that everyone is giving their best. That's how a team grows."

And in the ultra-tough Western Conference of the NHL, that's also how a team wins — by pushing one another to be their best.

HOCKEY MEMORY

It's not likely Joe will ever forget the 2005–2006 season: he was traded by the Boston Bruins (the team that drafted him) after more than seven seasons. He then led his new team, San Jose, and the NHL in scoring. He went on to be named the Hart Trophy winner as the NHL's MVP. It's the only time in NHL history that a player has won the scoring title and the Hart Trophy the year he was traded.

DID YOU KNOW?

Last season Joe missed a game on March 28 with a lower body injury. It was the first game he had missed since being traded to the Sharks on November 30, 2005 — a streak of 379 consecutive games.

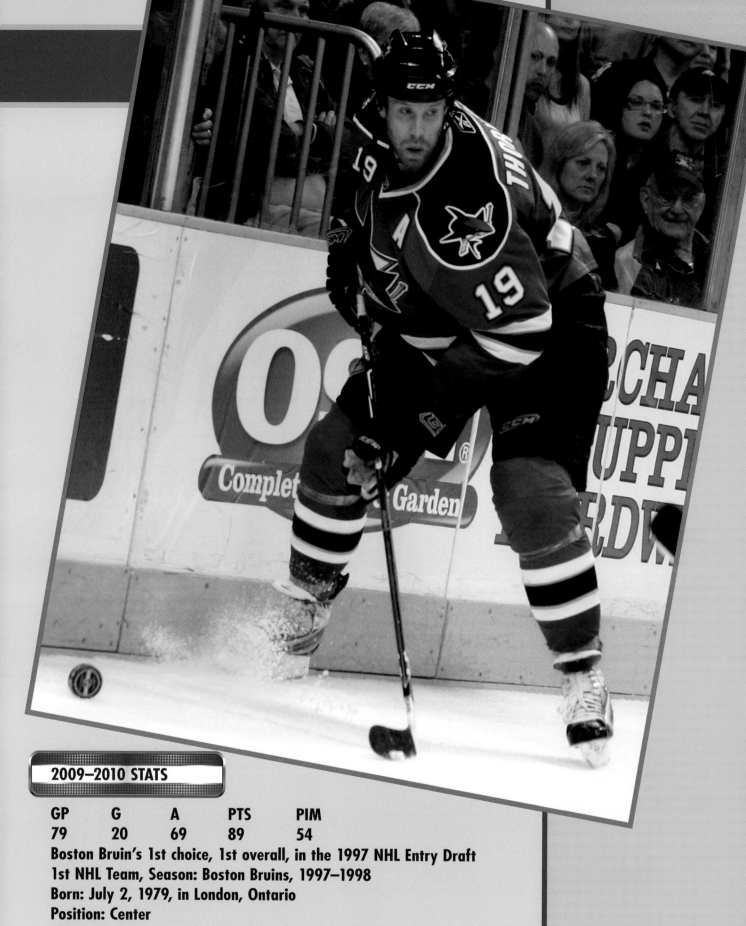

2009–2010 STATS

GP	G	A	PTS	PIM
79	20	69	89	54

Boston Bruin's 1st choice, 1st overall, in the 1997 NHL Entry Draft
1st NHL Team, Season: Boston Bruins, 1997–1998
Born: July 2, 1979, in London, Ontario
Position: Center
Shoots: Left
Height: 1.93 m (6'4")
Weight: 107 kg (235 lbs.)

REFEREE SIGNALS

Do you know what is happening when the referee stops play and makes a penalty call? If you don't, then you're missing an important part of the game. The referee can call different penalties that result in anything from playing a man short for two minutes to having a player kicked out of the game.

Here are some of the most common referee signals. Now you'll know what penalties are being called against your team.

Boarding
Checking an opponent into the boards in a violent way.

Charging
Checking an opponent in a violent way as a result of skating or charging at him.

Cross-checking
Striking an opponent with the stick, while both hands are on the stick and both arms are extended.

Elbowing
Checking an opponent with an elbow.

High-sticking
Striking an opponent with the stick, which is held above shoulder height.

Holding
Holding back an opponent with the hands or arms.

Hooking
Using the blade of the stick to hold back an opponent.

Icing
Shooting the puck across the opposing team's goal line from one's own side of the rink. Called only if the opposing player touches the puck first.

Interference
Holding back an opponent who does not have the puck in play.

Kneeing
Using a knee to hold back an opponent.

Misconduct
A ten-minute penalty — the longest type called. Usually for abuse of an official.

Roughing
Shoving or striking an opponent.

REFEREE SIGNALS

Slashing
Using the stick to strike an opponent.

Spearing
Poking an opponent with the blade of the stick.

Slow whistle
The official waits to blow his whistle because of a delayed offside or delayed penalty call. Done while the opposing team has control of the puck.

Tripping
Tripping an opponent with the stick, a hand or a foot.

Unsportsmanlike conduct
Showing poor sportsmanship toward an opponent. For example: biting, pulling hair, etc.

Wash-out
Goal not allowed.

Final Team Standings 2009–2010

EASTERN CONFERENCE

Atlantic Division

Team	GP	W	L	OT	PTS
NEW JERSEY	82	48	27	7	103
PITTSBURGH	82	47	28	7	101
PHILADELPHIA	82	41	35	6	88
NY RANGERS	82	38	33	11	87
NY ISLANDERS	82	34	37	11	79

Northeast Division

Team	GP	W	L	OT	PTS
BUFFALO	82	45	27	10	100
OTTAWA	82	44	32	6	94
BOSTON	82	39	30	13	91
MONTREAL	82	39	33	10	88
TORONTO	82	30	38	14	74

Southeast Division

Team	GP	W	L	OT	PTS
WASHINGTON	82	54	15	13	121
ATLANTA	82	35	34	13	83
CAROLINA	82	35	37	10	80
TAMPA BAY	82	34	36	12	80
FLORIDA	82	32	37	13	77

WESTERN CONFERENCE

Central Division

Team	GP	W	L	OT	PTS
CHICAGO	82	52	22	8	112
DETROIT	82	44	24	14	102
NASHVILLE	82	47	29	6	100
ST. LOUIS	82	40	32	10	90
COLUMBUS	82	32	35	15	79

Northwest Division

Team	GP	W	L	OT	PTS
VANCOUVER	82	49	28	5	103
COLORADO	82	43	30	9	95
CALGARY	82	40	32	10	90
MINNESOTA	82	38	36	8	84
EDMONTON	82	27	47	8	62

Pacific Division

Team	GP	W	L	OT	PTS
SAN JOSE	82	51	20	11	113
PHOENIX	82	50	25	7	107
LOS ANGELES	82	46	27	9	101
ANAHEIM	82	39	32	11	89
DALLAS	82	37	31	14	88

GP = Games played; W = Wins; L = Losses; OT = Overtime; PTS = Points

Top Ten Points Leaders 2009–2010

	PLAYER	TEAM	GP	G	A	P	S	S%
1	HENRIK SEDIN	VANCOUVER	82	29	83	112	166	17.5
2	SIDNEY CROSBY	PITTSBURGH	81	51	58	109	298	17.1
3	ALEX OVECHKIN	WASHINGTON	72	50	59	109	368	13.6
4	NICKLAS BACKSTROM	WASHINGTON	82	33	68	101	222	14.9
5	STEVEN STAMKOS	TAMPA BAY	82	51	44	95	297	17.2
6	MARTIN ST LOUIS	TAMPA BAY	82	29	65	94	242	12.0
7	BRAD RICHARDS	DALLAS	80	24	67	91	284	8.5
8	JOE THORNTON	SAN JOSE	79	20	69	89	141	14.2
9	PATRICK KANE	CHICAGO	82	30	58	88	261	11.5
10	MARIAN GABORIK	NY RANGERS	76	42	44	86	272	15.4

GP = Games played; G = Goals; A = Assists; P = Points;
S = Shots; S% = Percentage

Top Ten Goalies — Total Wins 2009–2010

	PLAYER	TEAM	GP	W	L	OT	SA%	GA	GAA
1	MARTIN BRODEUR	NEW JERSEY	77	45	25	6	.916	168	2.24
2	EVGENI NABOKOV	SAN JOSE	71	44	16	10	.922	170	2.43
3	IIYA BRYZGALOV	PHOENIX	69	42	20	6	.920	156	2.29
4	RYAN MILLER	BUFFALO	69	41	18	8	.929	150	2.22
5	ROBERTO LUONGO	VANCOUVER	68	40	22	4	.913	167	2.57
6	JONATHAN QUICK	LOS ANGELES	72	39	24	7	.907	180	2.54
7	CRAIG ANDERSON	COLORADO	71	38	25	7	.917	186	2.64
8	JIMMY HOWARD	DETROIT	63	37	15	10	.924	141	2.26
9	MARC-ANDRE FLEURY	PITTSBURGH	67	37	21	6	.905	168	2.65
10	MIIKKA KIPRUSOFF	CALGARY	73	35	28	10	.920	163	2.31

GP = Games played; W = Wins; L = Losses; OT = Overtime and/or Shut-Out Losses;
SA% = Save percentage; GA = Goals Against; GAA = Goals-Against Average

END-OF-SEASON STATS

Countdown to the Cup 2010–2011

EASTERN CONFERENCE

islander

backhauks

sharks

Daucks

kings

Comics

coyotes

stars

islander

Ducks

kings

stars

islander

stars

THE CHAMPION:

CUP FINAL

CONFERENCE FINAL

CONFERENCE SEMI-FINALS

CONFERENCE QUARTER-FINALS

THE CHAMPION:

Devils

3 Devils

3 Devils

Pathers

Devils

0 Rangers

5 Lighting

Pathers

Pens

Pens

Wilders

9 Wilders

Philyers

cups

9 Wilders

Wilders

**CONFERENCE
FINAL**

**CONFERENCE
SEMI-FINALS**

**CONFERENCE
QUARTER-FINALS**

NHL AWARDS

Here are some of the major NHL awards for individual players. Fill in your selection for each award and then fill in the name of the actual winner of the trophy.

HART MEMORIAL TROPHY

Awarded to the player judged to be the most valuable to his team. Selected by the Professional Hockey Writers Association.

2010 winner: **Henrik Sedin**

Your choice for 2011: _____

The winner: _____

ART ROSS TROPHY

Awarded to the player who leads the league in scoring points at the end of the regular season.

2010 winner: **Henrik Sedin**

Your choice for 2011: _____

The winner: _____

CALDER MEMORIAL TROPHY

Awarded to the player selected as the most proficient in his first year of competition in the NHL. Selected by the Professional Hockey Writers Association.

2010 winner: **Tyler Myers**

Your choice for 2011: _____

The winner: _____

JAMES NORRIS TROPHY

Awarded to the defense player who demonstrates throughout his season the greatest all-round ability. Selected by the Professional Hockey Writers Association.

2010 winner: **Duncan Keith**

Your choice for 2011: _____

The winner: _____

VEZINA TROPHY

Awarded to the goalkeeper judged to be the best. Selected by the NHL general managers.

2010 winner: **Ryan Miller**

Your choice for 2011: _____

The winner: _____

MAURICE RICHARD TROPHY

Awarded to the player who scores the highest number of regular-season goals.

2010 winner: **Sidney Crosby and Steven Stamkos**

Your choice for 2011: _____

The winner: _____

WILLIAM M. JENNINGS TROPHY

Awarded to the goalkeeper(s) who played a minimum of 25 games for the team with the fewest goals scored against it.

2010 winner: **Martin Brodeur**

Your choice for 2011: _____

The winner: _____

LADY BYNG MEMORIAL TROPHY

Awarded to the player judged to have exhibited the best sportsmanship combined with a high standard of playing ability. Selected by the Professional Hockey Writers Association.

2010 winner: **Martin St. Louis**

Your choice for 2011: _____

The winner: _____

FRANK J. SELKE TROPHY

Awarded to the forward who best excels in the defensive aspects of the game. Selected by the Professional Hockey Writers Association.

2010 winner: **Pavel Datsyuk**

Your choice for 2011: _____

The winner: _____

CONN SMYTHE TROPHY

Awarded to the player most valuable to his team in the Stanley Cup Playoffs. Selected by the Professional Hockey Writers Association.

2010 winner: **Jonathan Toews**

Your choice for 2011: _____

The winner: _____

BILL MASTERTON MEMORIAL TROPHY

Awarded to the player who best exemplifies the qualitites of perseverance, sportsmanship and dedication to hockey. Selected by the Professional Hockey Writers Association.

2010 winner: **Jose Theodore**

Your choice for 2011: _____

The winner: _____

To Cindy — a First Team All-Star sister
and a great mom.

— P. R.

Illustrations by Bill Dickson

Photo credits:
Sidney Crosby: Getty Images/Bruce Bennett
Drew Doughty: NHLI via Getty Images/Jamie Sabau
Mike Fisher: Getty Images/Joel Auerbach
Marian Gaborik: Getty Images/Nick Laham
Jaroslav Halak, Patrick Kane, Evgeni Malkin,
Alex Ovechkin: Getty Images/Jim McIsaac
Jarome Iginla: Getty Images/Paul Bereswill
Roberto Luongo: NHLI via Getty Images/ Jeff Vinnick
Patrick Marleau: Getty Images/Jeff Gross
Ryan Miller, Zach Parise: NHLI via Getty Images/Andy Marlin
Brad Richards: NHLI via Getty Images/Glenn James
Henrik Sedin: NHLI via Getty Images/ Noah Graham
Joe Thornton: Getty Images/ Jed Jacobsohn

ISBN 978-1-4431-0278-0

6 5 4 3 2 1   Printed in Canada 118   10 11 12 13 14

Mixed Sources
Product group from well-managed forests
and other controlled sources
www.fsc.org   Cert no. SW-COC-000952
©1996 Forest Stewardship Council
FSC